It's Not About You, Mrs. Turkey

A Love Letter About
the True Meaning of Thanksgiving

Soraya Diase Coffelt
Illustrated by Tea Seroya

The Love Letters Book Series

NEW YORK

It's Not About You, Mrs. Turkey
A Love Letter About the True Meaning of Thanksgiving

© 2016 Soraya Diase Coffelt. Illustrated by Tea Seroya.

All rights reserved. No portion of this book may be reproduced, stored in a retrieval system, or transmitted in any form or by any means—electronic, mechanical, photocopy, recording, scanning, or other—except for brief quotations in critical reviews or articles, without the prior written permission of the publisher.

Published in New York, New York, by Morgan James Publishing. Morgan James and The Entrepreneurial Publisher are trademarks of Morgan James, LLC. www.MorganJamesPublishing.com

The Morgan James Speakers Group can bring authors to your live event. For more information or to book an event visit The Morgan James Speakers Group at www.TheMorganJames-SpeakersGroup.com.

Scripture quotations are taken from the Holy Bible, New Living Translation, copyright ©1996, 2004, 2007 by Tyndale House Foundation. Used by permission of Tyndale House Publishers, Inc., Carol Stream, Illinois 60188. All rights reserved.

A **free** eBook edition is available with the purchase of this print book.

ISBN 978-1-63047-636-6 paperback
ISBN 978-1-63047-637-3 eBook
ISBN 978-1-63047-637-3 hardcover
Library of Congress Control Number: 2015906531

CLEARLY PRINT YOUR NAME ABOVE IN UPPER CASE

Instructions to claim your free eBook edition:
1. Download the BitLit app for Android or iOS
2. Write your name in **UPPER CASE** on the line
3. Use the BitLit app to submit a photo
4. Download your eBook to any device

In an effort to support local communities and raise awareness and funds, Morgan James Publishing donates a percentage of all book sales for the life of each book to Habitat for Humanity Peninsula and Greater Williamsburg.

Get involved today, visit
www.MorganJamesBuilds.com

Habitat for Humanity™
Peninsula and
Greater Williamsburg
Building Partner

I dedicate this book to my loving mother Josefina Diase. She taught me to read at a very early age, establishing one of the important foundations for my life. She made so many sacrifices for me and I can never thank her enough for all she has done. What a great mother I have been blessed with!

God told Abraham that because of his faithfulness, God would bless him and all of his descendants, who would be as numerous as the stars of the sky.
Genesis 15:5; 22:15; Hebrews 11:8-12.

Children, along with adults, are among Abraham's descendants.

It's Not About You, Mrs. Turkey

Dear Mrs. Turkey,

Thanksgiving Day is one of my most favorite holidays! Of course, you are the "star" that day in lots of places in the United States, and you sure do taste great, but a turkey is not what Thanksgiving Day is truly about. Thanksgiving is made up of two words—"thanks" and "giving"—and that's what my letter to you explains.

I'm a kid who loves to eat. And what's the best day of the year to eat, and Eat, and EAT? You guessed it—Thanksgiving Day!

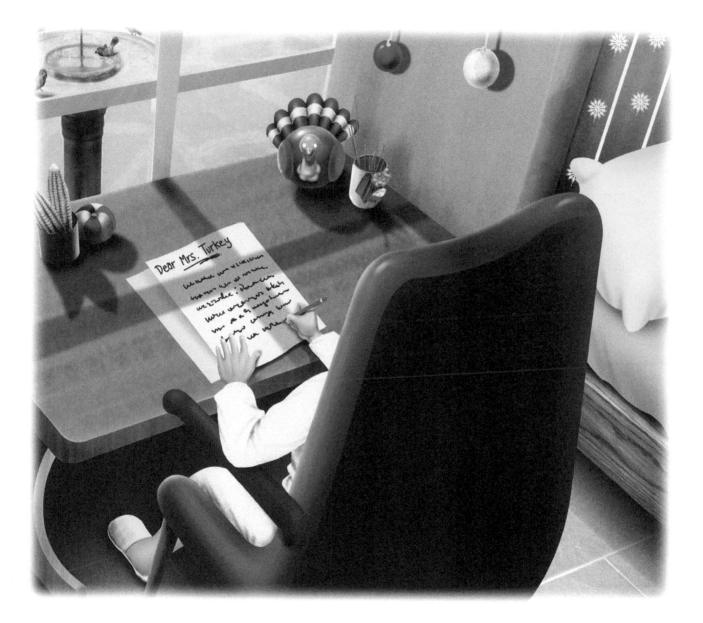

On that day, a lot of our family members and friends come to our house. From early in the morning until late at night, we eat…and Eat…AND EAT. And right at the center of attention is the turkey! My mom rubs some special seasoning on it the night before. Then, she wakes up early in the morning to put it in the oven to bake slowly. All day we smell it cooking, along with the trimmings of mashed potatoes, yams, gravy, and corn. I think my favorite part is the amazing desserts—pies, sweetbreads, cookies, and lots of other goodies!

You name it and we probably have it to eat that day. I gobble down so much food that my belly gets S-O-O-O F-U-L-L! Wow! I'm getting hungry right now just thinking about it as I write this letter to you!

By the way, did you notice that I wrote the word "gobble" just now? Ha ha! That was smart of me, wasn't it, since turkeys are known for making "gobble" noises.

It's awesome that you provide such yummy food for us to eat, Mrs. Turkey. And from what I just said of our Thanksgiving Day, it certainly seems that the celebration of this wonderful holiday is all about you. But even though you are a very special part (that I really enjoy!), Thanksgiving isn't all about food! There is so much more to this holiday. It's an amazing story of courage and faith that I'm going to tell you about.

It all began many, many years ago, way back around 1600. A group of people named the Pilgrims lived in England. They loved God and wanted to worship Him freely without any restrictions. But, instead, they were arrested, put in jail, and punished when they worshiped God. So God gave them the idea to move across the Atlantic Ocean to live in the New World where they would be free to pray to God and worship Him. I think that was very brave of them. They left everything they had because of their love for God and their trust in Him!

The New World was the name given to what we now know as the United States of America. This was long before there were cars or planes, so the Pilgrims had to sail across a huge ocean on a ship. It wasn't easy, but they escaped England on a ship named the Mayflower. In all, there were about 102 Pilgrims who made the trip. And guess what? There were 32 kids on that ship too! Kids are very important to God (and their moms and dads) so they weren't left behind.

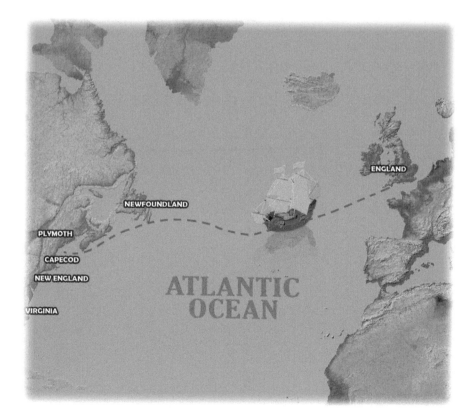

The ship sailed from England in the late part of the summer in 1620. It was a very long trip over the Atlantic Ocean and the weather was bad for much of it. The seas were rough, the winds were strong, and the waves crashed against the ship. Many people got sick. But, they didn't turn back. They knew that God wanted them to come to America and they believed that He would protect them.

On the ship, the Pilgrims got together and made an agreement called the Mayflower Compact. The Compact explained that they were traveling to America for the glory of God and because they were Christians. It said that they planned to establish a colony where people could live for God and worship Him freely. Now they wouldn't have to be afraid anymore to go to church or to talk and sing about God. As part of the Compact, they agreed to treat each other equally and to elect leaders who were godly men.

On a cold November morning in 1620, the ship landed at what is now Cape Cod in the state of Massachusetts. Do you know where Massachusetts is, Mrs. Turkey? If you look at a map of the United States, you'll find it in the northeast part of the country, bordering the Atlantic Ocean.

On the first Sunday that they were in America, the Pilgrims spent the day praying and thanking God for the safe voyage across the Atlantic Ocean.

13

At that time, the Indians were living in the New World. They had many different tribes and cities already established. They were great hunters, fishermen, and gatherers. They were also good farmers and grew a lot of plants for food. One of the vegetables they grew was corn. This was something new to the Pilgrims. I sure do like to eat corn on the cob with lots of butter! Yum-yum!

When the Pilgrims arrived in the New World, they didn't know that there were Indians nearby. The Indian nation in that area was named Wampanoag. When some of the Pilgrim men got off the ship to explore, they found a few Indian homes and lots of corn, but the Indians hid from them.

The Pilgrims searched for a good place to build their homes, but they didn't stay at this first area. They got back on their ship and sailed further around until they came to an area that is now called Plymouth Harbor. The Pilgrims liked it there because it had a brook with fresh water and a high hill where they could keep a good lookout for anyone who might want to hurt them. This was to be their new home. They named the town Plymouth. But, the Pilgrims were about to find out that their journey to establish a new home had really just begun.

The first winter was very cold. Their food supplies, which they had brought with them, were getting really low. Some of the Pilgrims got sick and died. It was a very hard time for them. When spring finally came, an Indian named Samoset walked into their town. He spoke good English because he had lived with several Englishmen who had come to fish near his home. The Pilgrims were very surprised to see him and welcomed him.

Soon, Samoset came back and brought another Indian with him named Squanto. Squanto spoke very good English too. He taught the Pilgrims how to fish, farm the land, and hunt for deer and turkey. It was all very different for the Pilgrims in this new land than their homeland they had left.

The Pilgrims and the Indians were very different also. I'm sure the Indians thought that the Pilgrims wore funny-looking clothes and hats. (Although, I bet the Pilgrims didn't think that their clothes looked funny!) The Pilgrim men usually wore shirts with ruffles, pants to their knees, and high-topped boots. When they attended church, the Pilgrim men wore black clothes and black hats that were tall and thin. The ladies usually wore bonnets on their heads and long dresses with aprons down to their ankles.

If how the Pilgrims dressed looked funny to the Indians, I'm sure the Pilgrims thought that the Indians wore funny clothes too! (But the Indians probably didn't think their clothes were funny either.) They wore clothes made out of animal skins and fur. They also wore jewelry made out of shells and beads and painted their skin with all sorts of different colors and designs!

20

Squanto introduced the Wampanoag Indians to the Pilgrims. The two groups made a peace treaty in which they agreed to help each other. Even though the Indians and Pilgrims were so different, they still worked together and helped one another.

In the fall of 1621, the Pilgrims celebrated their first Thanksgiving, and it actually lasted about three days! They thanked God for all they had. Even though the past winter had been very cold, they were happy that they had made it through. Most of them were healthy. Their new town was growing. God had kept them safe and given the Indians as friends. They loved the Indians and the Indians loved them. The Pilgrims and the Indians shared what they had for food, like wild turkey, corn, and pumpkin. They played games and danced together, and had a lot of fun.

Many years later, in 1863, President Abraham Lincoln made a Thanksgiving proclamation. He said that he wanted all Americans to set apart the last Thursday in the month of November every year as a day of thanksgiving and praise to God for all that He has done for us and for all that He has given us. President Lincoln said that it was important that we never forget from where all our blessings come.

So that, Mrs. Turkey, is the true meaning of Thanksgiving Day. It is a day in which we remember the past and present and give thanks to the true God. It reminds us that we should always put Him first. So, while I love you, Mrs. Turkey, it's important to understand that Thanksgiving really isn't about you after all. But that's ok. I will still enjoy your part of the celebration and will remember to thank God for His provision as I eat, and Eat and EAT.

Love,

Me

Dear Reader,

If you want to celebrate Jesus and make Him Lord of your life, say this simple prayer:

"Dear Lord Jesus, thank you for loving me so much that You died on the cross for my sins. I ask you to be my Lord and Savior.

Amen."

About the Author

Soraya Diase Coffelt is a widow and the mother of two sons. She is a lawyer and former judge of the Territorial Court of the Virgin Islands (now renamed the Superior Court) on St. Thomas, U.S. Virgin Islands. She began as a parent volunteer in the Children's Ministry at her church, and over a period of about 15 years, became a leader and then a lay minister in the Children's Ministry. She has been on missionary trips to Honduras and the Amazon Region of Peru ministering to adults and children. God has given her many creative ideas for ministering His Word to children, and her books are among some of them.

In 2012, she established a non-profit foundation, As the Stars of the Sky Foundation, Inc., to assist with the physical and spiritual needs of children. All proceeds from the sale of her books go towards the foundation.

If you have enjoyed this book and want to learn more about Jesus' life, I invite you to purchase a copy of another book in The Love Letters series:

It's Not About You, Mr. Pumpkin

It's Not About You, Mr. Santa Claus

And more….

To order your copy, please go to:

www.asthestarsofthesky.org

or email us: info@asthestarsofthesky.org

CPSIA information can be obtained at www.ICGtesting.com
Printed in the USA
LVOW05s0234060815

448985LV00003B/4/P